That's The Power
Surrounds Me
Freedom
Hope Of The Ages
Never Walk Alone
Resurrender
Secret Place
Song For His Presence
All To Him

Hillsong Worship

Hillsong Worship exists to serve the global church and equip believers everywhere with songs of Holy Spirit power that exalt and glorify the Name of Jesus, build the church and fuel revival on the earth. Songs such as "King of Kings," "Cornerstone," "Mighty to Save," "This I Believe (The Creed)," "Who You Say I Am" and the Grammy award winning, "What A Beautiful Name" have been adopted by believers around the world, bringing new expression to the faith and hope we have as Christians. Resourcing the church has long been at the heart of Hillsong Worship, whether through songs and sheet music, or instrument parts and translations. Featuring worship leaders and songwriters such as Brooke Ligertwood, Ben Fielding, Reuben Morgan, Joel Houston, Taya Gaukrodger, Hannah Hobbs, David Ware and more, Hillsong Worship is committed to continuing its legacy of writing and leading songs that by God's grace, impact both individual devotion and congregational worship for the glory of God.

United, Y&F and Hillsong Kids Teams

United is committed to writing songs that speak truth, create a unique sound, connect with churches, individuals and ultimately connect people everywhere with God. Young & Free (Y&F) is the creative worship expression of Hillsong Church's current youth movement. When on tour, both United and Young & Free are accompanied by the whole Hillsong team's support and prayers that their ministry would arrest hearts and point people to Jesus, impacting individuals, local youth groups and local churches. United and Y&F teams also serve as part of Hillsong Worship and our worship and creative team. Hillsong Kids is the children's ministry of Hillsong Church, creating moments kids will never forget as they grow in faith through Christ Jesus.

We are a church committed to inspiring and empowering the authentic worship of Jesus and resourcing the body of Christ.

There are numerous resources we as Hillsong make available including inspiring teaching and books by Brian & Bobbie Houston, curriculum content that can impact your children, outreach and discipleship ministries and of course music. For more information visit hillsongmusic.com

We are a church that believes in championing the cause of the local church.

Hillsong conference is about you, your church and seeing God's kingdom advance across the earth. This is your chance to lean in, receive and take home practical teachings you can outwork in your own church home, family and community. It's about being refreshed and inspired and finding great strength and unity amongst the diversity of the local church worldwide. For more information visit hillsong.com/conference

We are a church that believes in placing value upon womanhood.

Colour Conference at the very core is a strong humanitarian message. Our passion and labour is to place value upon womanhood, so that we in turn can arise from a place of strength and cohesion and place value upon fellow humanity. For more information visit hillsong.com/colour

We are a church that believes in reaching and influencing the world with the message of Jesus Christ.

Hillsong channel is an innovative media movement, beaming the timeless message of Jesus around the globe into television screens and digital devices to empower people in every sphere of life. This is a platform positioned in the heart of culture bringing Jesus into prisons and palaces all over the world. For more information visit hillsong.com/channel

Hillsong television with Brian Houston is a half-hour Christian television program that features his teaching from Hillsong Church services. Pastor Brian's messages are empowering, passionate and practical for everyday life. His teaching will inspire you with the hope, joy, meaning and purpose that can be found in a personal and loving God. For more information visit hillsong.com/tv

We are a church that believes in partnership and unity as we advance His kingdom on earth.

The hillsong leadership network is all about connecting, equipping and serving leaders and exists to champion the cause of local churches everywhere. Our heart is that by coming alongside leaders, churches and ministries of varying denominations and styles, we are able to see more churches flourish and reach their God-given potential through this membership program. For more information visit hillsong.com/network

We are a church that believes in equipping people with principles and tools to lead and impact in every sphere of life.

To find further information about the pastoral leadership streams (including youth, children, event management, or social justice pathways), creative streams (including worship music, tv & media, dance and production) or a degree program offered on campus by Alphacrucis College visit hillsong.com/college

We are a church in many locations.

Asia Pacific Australia, Fiji, Indonesia, **Europe** Austria, Denmark, France, Germany, Italy, Netherlands, Norway, Portugal, Russia, Spain, Sweden, Switzerland, Ukraine, United Kingdom **North America** Canada, USA **Latin America** Argentina, Brazil, Mexico, Uruguay **Africa & Middle East** Kenya, Mauritius, South Africa, Israel **Online** Online Campus, Church of the Air. For service times and information visit hillsong.com

Our prayer

Our prayer is that you would discover the author of love... The Lord Jesus Christ. His life and death represent the greatest gift of love the world will ever see... "This is real love—not that we loved God, but that he loved us and sent his son as a sacrifice to take away our sins." (1 John 4:10 NLT) God paid the ultimate sacrifice sending His Son, Jesus Christ, who died on the cross in our place and rose again to prove His victory, restore us to relationship with Him and empower us for life. It is through Jesus Christ that we can know and be reconciled with God... All we need to do is believe in Him and accept Jesus Christ as our Lord and Saviour. It is as simple as praying a prayer... Asking Jesus to meet you right where you are... It is a brand new start of living in relationship with God... If you are not sure that you personally know the Lord Jesus, we would like to encourage you to make this your prayer today:

Dear Lord Jesus, thank You for dying on the cross for me. Thank You for Your amazing love. I repent of my sins and thank You for Your forgiveness. Please come into my life and give me a fresh start. I believe in You and accept You as my Lord and Saviour. I am now a Christian – a follower of Jesus Christ and You now live in me. Help me to live my life for You from this day forward. Amen.

If you have prayed this prayer today, we would love to hear from you! Please write to us at: Hillsong Church, PO Box 1195, Castle Hill, NSW 1765, Australia or email us at: prayer@hillsong.com

TERMS AND CONDITIONS

Thank you for purchasing sheet music from Hillsong Music. Your purchase grants you the right to make ONE copy of the sheet music for your personal purposes (performances, worship services, personal study, musical recording, etc). However the following rights have NOT been granted to you:
1. Reproduce copies of this sheet music in whole or in part outside of the rights granted to you above.
2. To translate, enhance, modify, alter or forge the sheet music or any part of it for any purpose.
3. Cause or permit any third party to translate, enhance, modify, alter or adapt the sheet music or any part of it for any purpose.
4. Sub-license, lease, lend, sell, rent, distribute or grant others any rights, or provide copies of the sheet music to others. Reproductions of the sheet music can be made for the purpose of church worship only with an existing Music Reproduction Licence from CCLI. For further information contact CCLI at http://www.ccli.com

For further information about copyright or other use of this music, please contact Hillsong Music Publishing at publisher.gsn@hillsong.com

TRANSCRIBED & ENGRAVED BY JARED HASCHEK

THAT'S THE POWER

Words and Music by
MICHAEL FATKIN, BENJAMIN HASTINGS
& ALEXANDER PAPPAS

© 2021 Hillsong Music Publishing Australia. CCLI: 7177422
All rights reserved. International copyright secured. Used by permission.
Tel: +61 2 8853 5284 Email: publishing@hillsong.com

THAT'S THE POWER

Words and Music by
MICHAEL FATKIN, BENJAMIN HASTINGS
& ALEXANDER PAPPAS

There's a Name that lev - els moun - tains,
There's a faith that stands de - fi - ant,

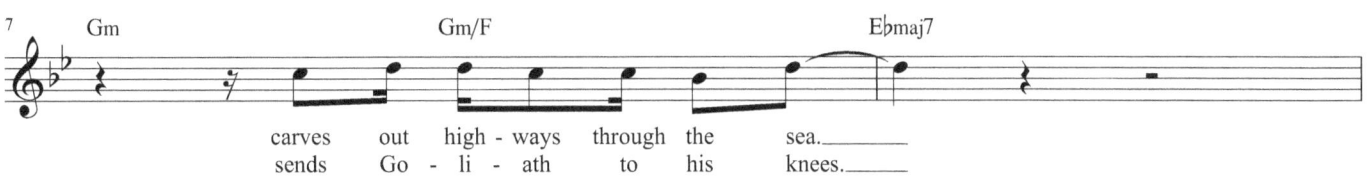

carves out high - ways through the sea.
sends Go - li - ath to his knees.

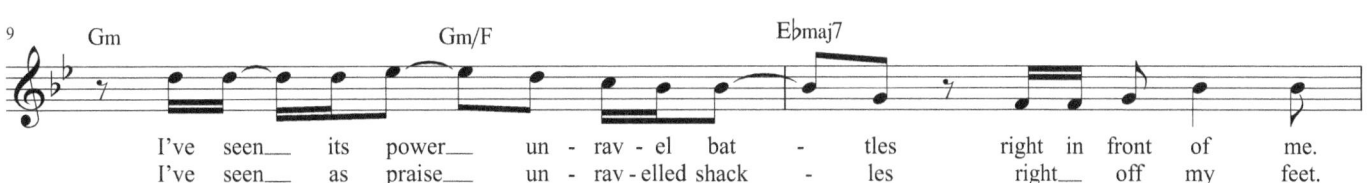

I've seen its power un - rav - el bat - tles right in front of me.
I've seen as praise un - rav - elled shack - les right off my feet.

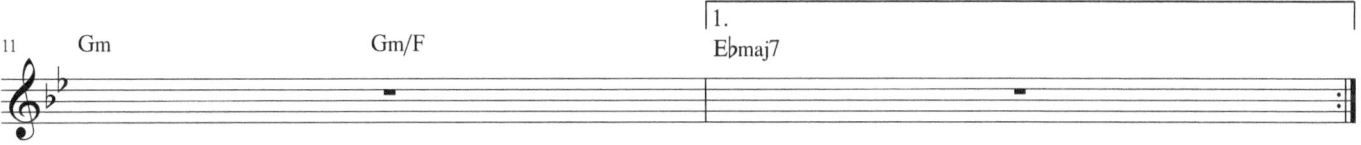

© 2021 Hillsong Music Publishing Australia. CCLI: 7177422
All rights reserved. International copyright secured. Used by permission.
Tel: +61 2 8853 5284 Email: publishing@hillsong.com

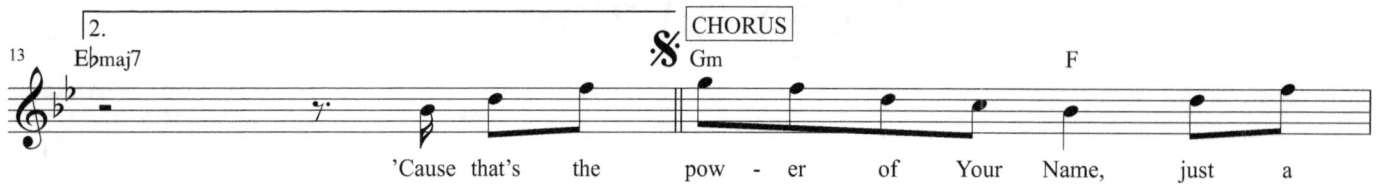
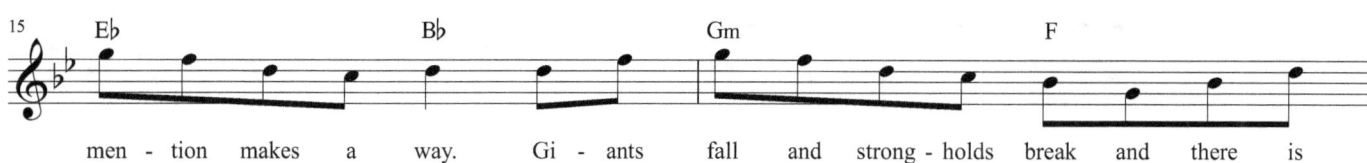

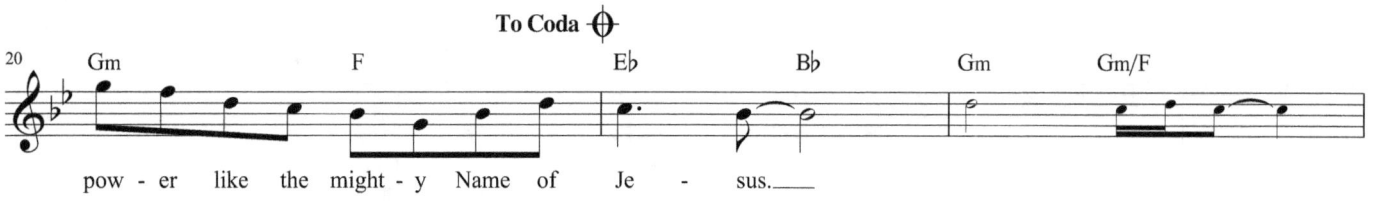

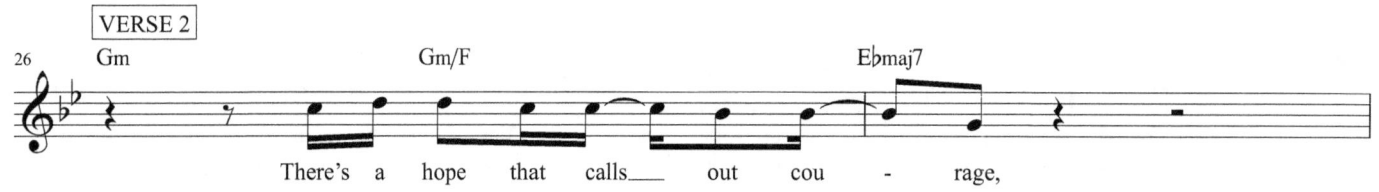

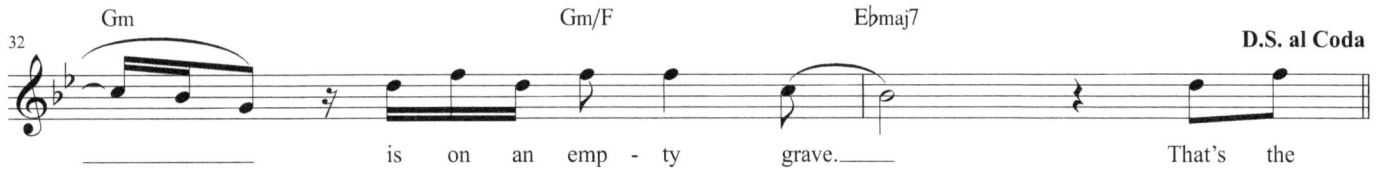

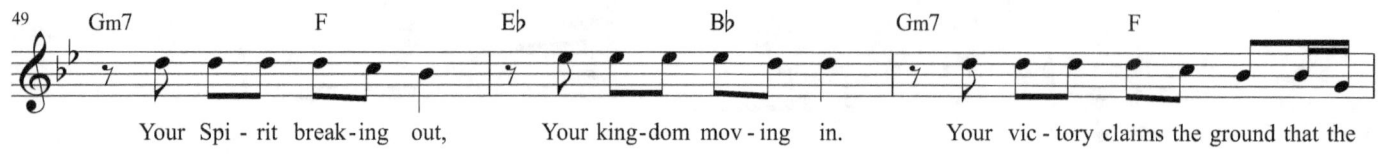

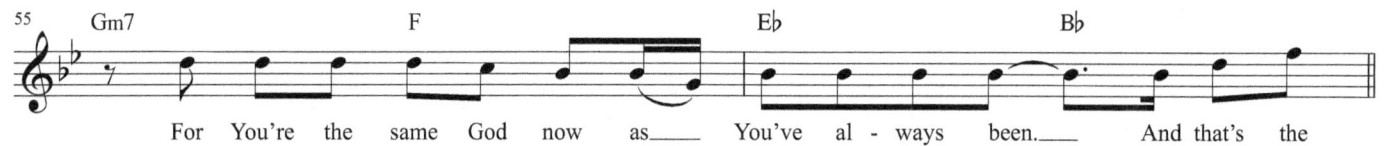
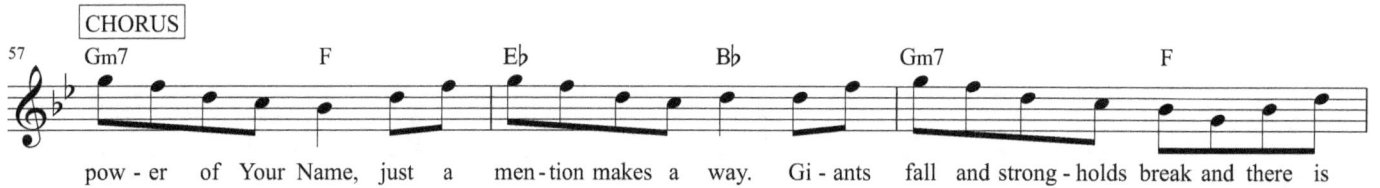

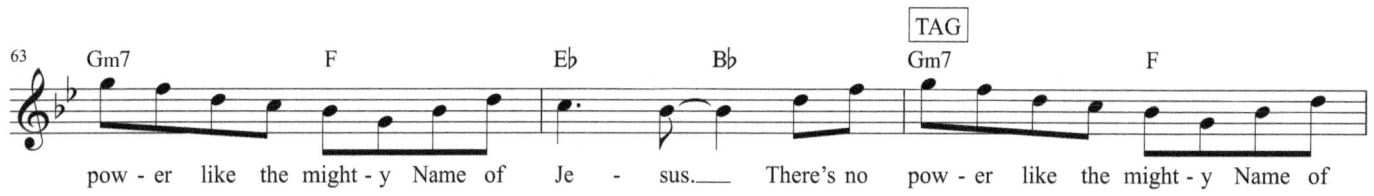

THAT'S THE POWER

**Words and Music by
Michael Fatkin, Benjamin Hastings &
Alexander Pappas**

VERSE 1:
There's a Name that levels mountains
Carves out highways through the sea
I've seen its power unravel battles
Right in front of me

There's a faith that stands defiant
Sends Goliath to his knees
I've seen as praise unravelled shackles
Right off my feet

CHORUS:
That's the power of Your Name
Just a mention makes a way
Giants fall and strongholds break
And there is healing

That's the power that I claim
It's the same that rolled the grave
There's no power like the
Mighty Name of Jesus

© 2021 Hillsong Music Publishing Australia
CCLI: 7177422

PO Box 1195 Castle Hill NSW 1765
Ph: +61 2 8853 5284 Fx: +61 2 8846 4625
E-mail: publishing@hillsong.com

That's The Power – Page 2

VERSE 2:
There's a hope that calls out courage
In the furnace unafraid
The kind of daring expectation
That every prayer I make
Is on an empty grave

BRIDGE:
I see You taking ground
I see You press ahead
Your power is dangerous to
The enemy's camp

You still do miracles
You will do what You said
For You're the same God now as
You've always been

Your Spirit breaking out
Your kingdom moving in
Your victory claims the ground that
The enemy had

You still do miracles
You will do what You said
For You're the same God now as
You've always been

© 2021 Hillsong Music Publishing Australia
CCLI: 7177422

PO Box 1195 Castle Hill NSW 1765
Ph: +61 2 8853 5284 Fx: +61 2 8846 4625
E-mail: publishing@hillsong.com

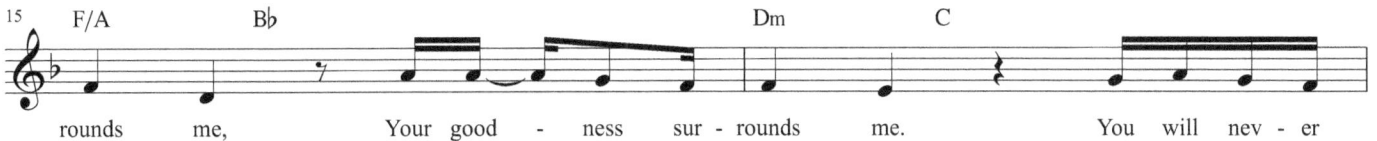
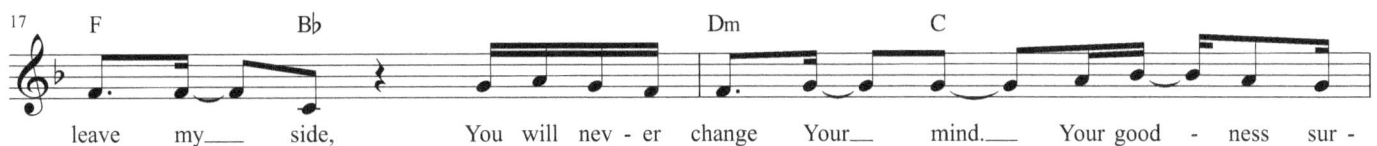
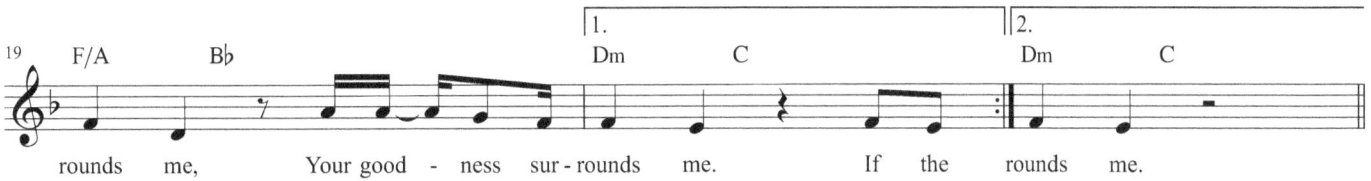
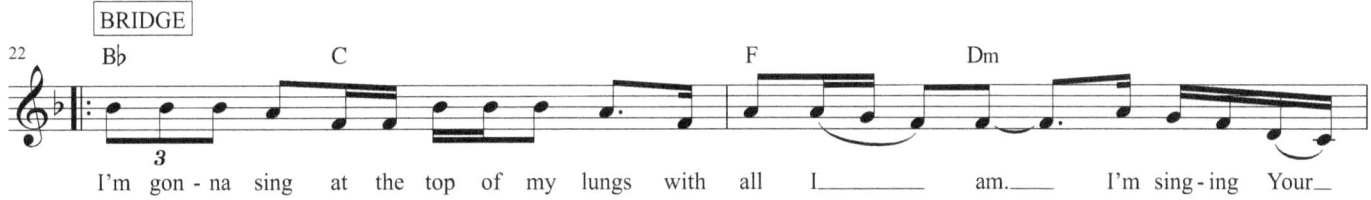

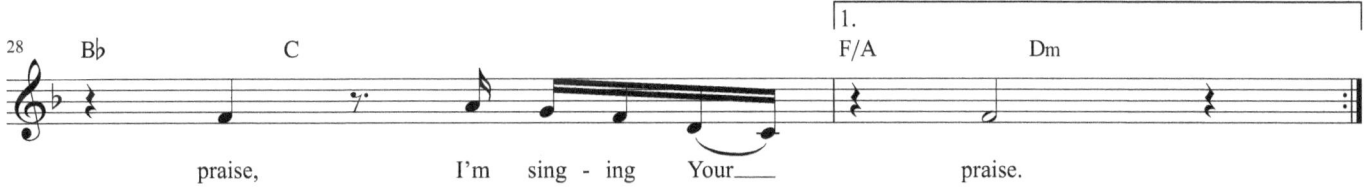

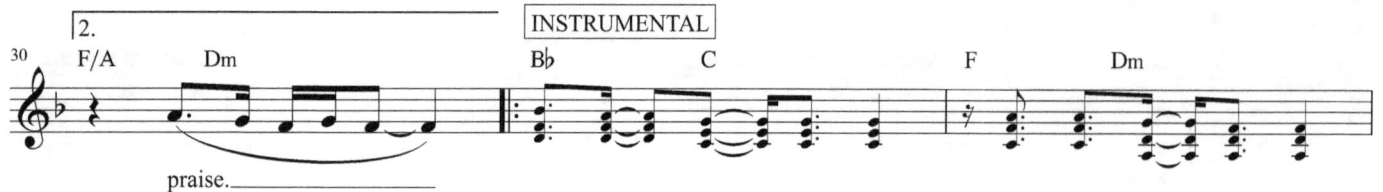

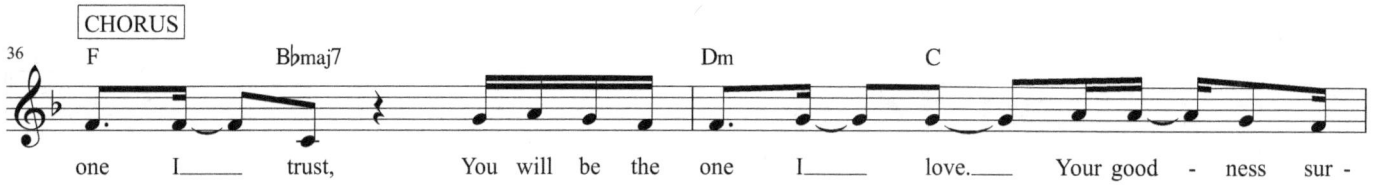
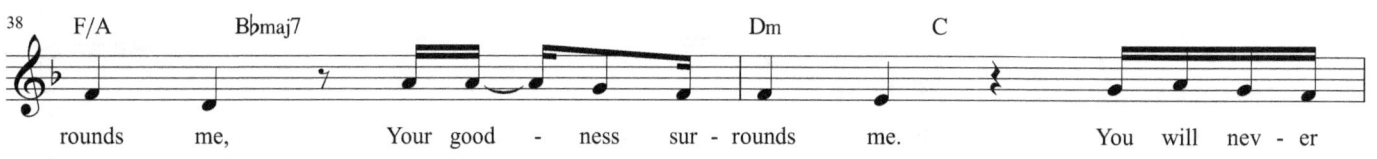
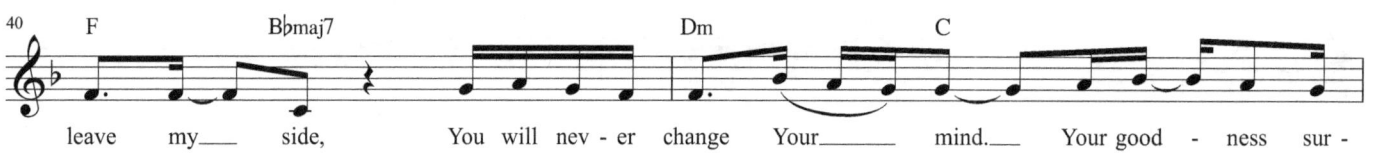

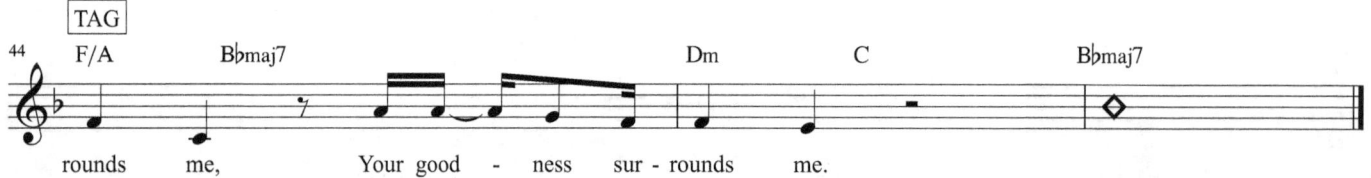

SURROUNDS ME

**Words and Music by
Reuben Morgan & Sarah Griffiths**

VERSE 1:
You have searched my heart oh God
You have known my ways
Every detail and every thought
You reveal Your grace
And call me deeper

CHORUS:
You will be the one I trust
You will be the one I love
Your goodness surrounds me
Your goodness surrounds me

You will never leave my side
You will never change Your mind
Your goodness surrounds me
Your goodness surrounds me

© 2021 Hillsong Music Publishing Australia &
Universal Songs Of PolyGram Int., Inc. (BMI)
CCLI: 7184445

PO Box 1195 Castle Hill NSW 1765
Ph: +61 2 8853 5284 Fx: +61 2 8846 4625
E-mail: publishing@hillsong.com

VERSE 2:
If the night brings a troubled heart
Will You meet me there
You light up every road I run
All Your plans are good
You're always faithful

BRIDGE:
I'm gonna sing at the top of my lungs
With all I am
I'm singing Your praise
I'm singing Your praise

I'm gonna sing at the top of my lungs
I won't hold back
I'm singing Your praise
I'm singing Your praise

© 2021 Hillsong Music Publishing Australia &
Universal Songs Of PolyGram Int., Inc. (BMI)
CCLI: 7184445

PO Box 1195 Castle Hill NSW 1765
Ph: +61 2 8853 5284 Fx: +61 2 8846 4625
E-mail: publishing@hillsong.com

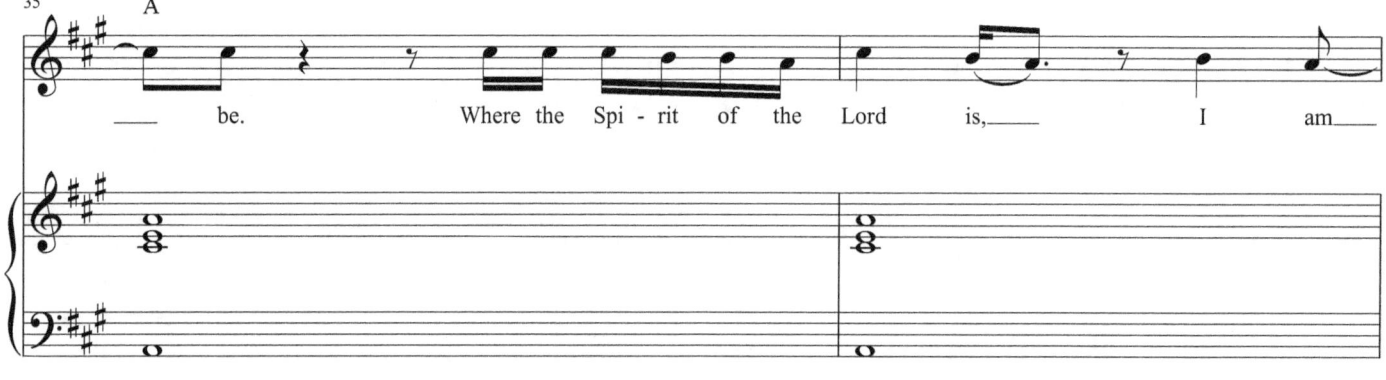

FREEDOM

**Words and Music by
Joshua Grimmett & Reuben Morgan**

VERSE 1:
My life is a prodigal story
Saved out of the enemy's plans for me
I'm home in the house of God
My life is a rescue story

CHORUS:
I have freedom
I have freedom
Thank You Jesus
I am free

No more chains on me
Now in Christ I live
Thank You Jesus
I am free

© 2021 Hillsong Music Publishing UK &
Hillsong Music Publishing Australia
CCLI: 7184448

PO Box 1195 Castle Hill NSW 1765
Ph: +61 2 8853 5284 Fx: +61 2 8846 4625
E-mail: publishing@hillsong.com

VERSE 2:
Our God is a jail breaker
Tears down unshakeable walls
Sing loud so all can hear us
He is unstoppable

BRIDGE:
Where the Spirit of the Lord is
There I will be
Where the Spirit of the Lord is
I am free

Where the presence of the Lord is
There I will be
Where the presence of the Lord is
I am free

HOPE OF THE AGES

Words and Music by
REUBEN MORGAN & CODY CARNES

Powerfully ♩. = 66

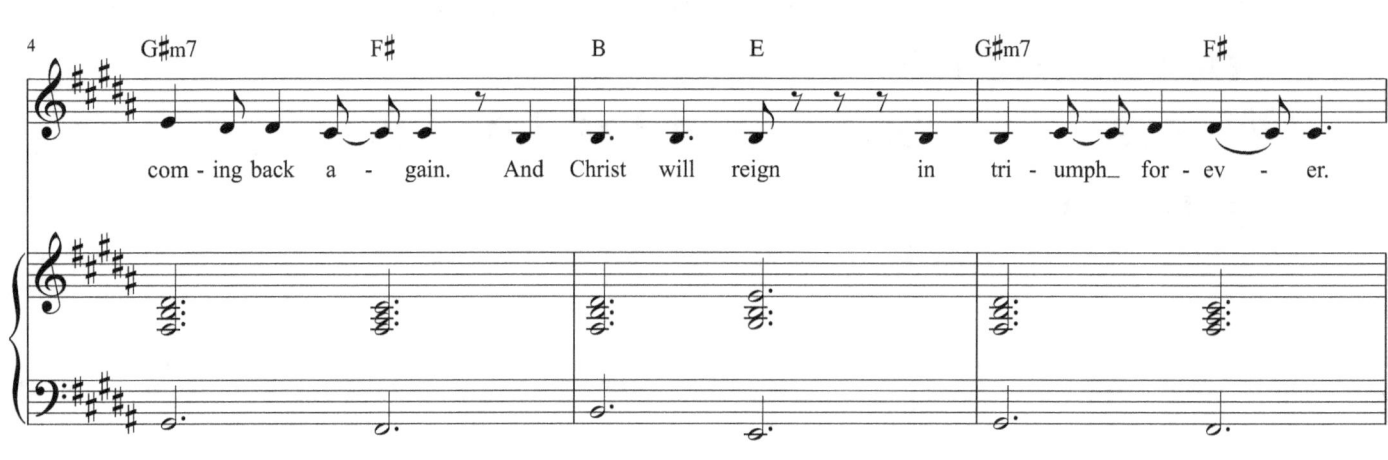

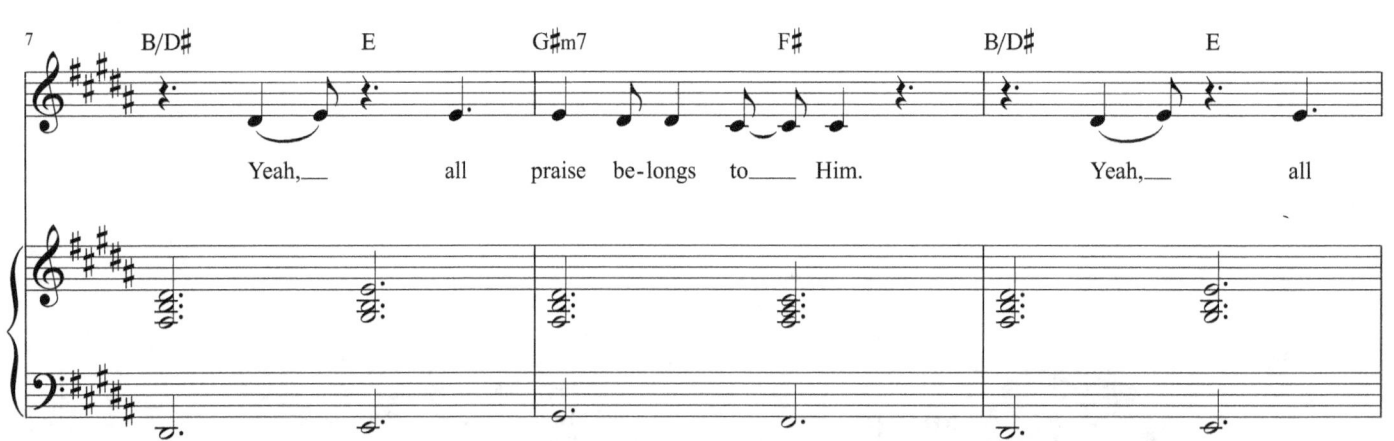

© 2021 Hillsong Music Publishing Australia & Capitol CMG Paragon / Writers Roof Publishing (BMI) (Admin. at CapitolCMGPublishing.com). CCLI: 7179458
All rights reserved. International copyright secured. Used by permission.
Tel: +61 2 8853 5284 Email: publishing@hillsong.com

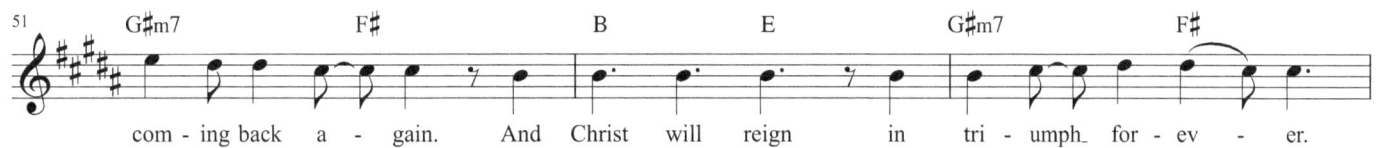

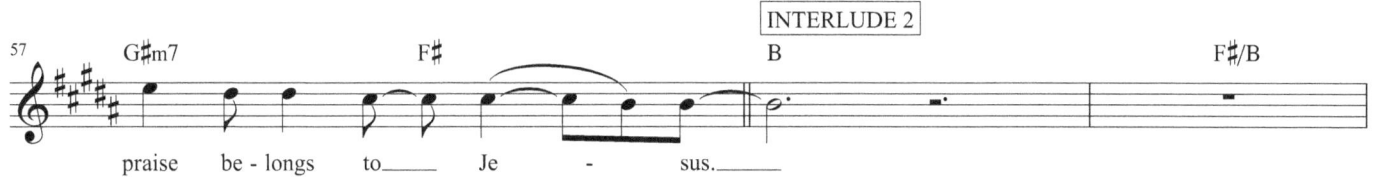
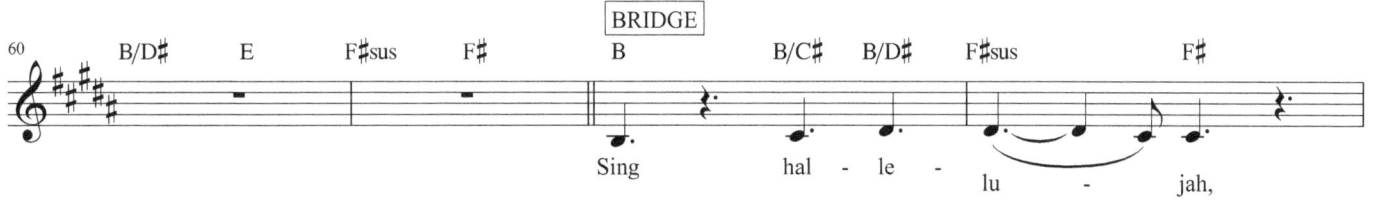

HOPE OF THE AGES

**Words and Music by
Reuben Morgan & Cody Carnes**

VERSE 1:
The gospel of Jesus
It's the hope of the ages
Burning brighter and brighter
And standing forever

The Church He is building
Nothing can stop it
It's a city that's shining
A light in the darkness

TAG:
Nothing can stop it

CHORUS:
Though Christ was dead
Now surely He's risen
Yeah He's coming back again

© 2021 Hillsong Music Publishing Australia & Capitol CMG
Paragon / Writers Roof Publishing (BMI) (Admin. at
CapitolCMGPublishing.com)
CCLI: 7179458
PO Box 1195 Castle Hill NSW 1765
Ph: +61 2 8853 5284 Fx: +61 2 8846 4625
E-mail: publishing@hillsong.com

And Christ will reign
In triumph forever
Yeah all praise belongs to Him
Yeah all praise belongs to Jesus

VERSE 2:
His Word is the answer
For all generations
It will never be tainted
It will never be broken

This is our confession
This is our conviction
We believe what is written
We believe what You've spoken

BRIDGE:
Sing hallelujah
Christ is our Redeemer
Shout hallelujah
Jesus holds our future

© 2021 Hillsong Music Publishing Australia & Capitol CMG Paragon / Writers Roof Publishing (BMI) (Admin. at CapitolCMGPublishing.com)

CCLI: 7179458

PO Box 1195 Castle Hill NSW 1765
Ph: +61 2 8853 5284 Fx: +61 2 8846 4625
E-mail: publishing@hillsong.com

NEVER WALK ALONE

**Words and Music by
BEN FIELDING, HANNAH HOBBS
& JENN JOHNSON**

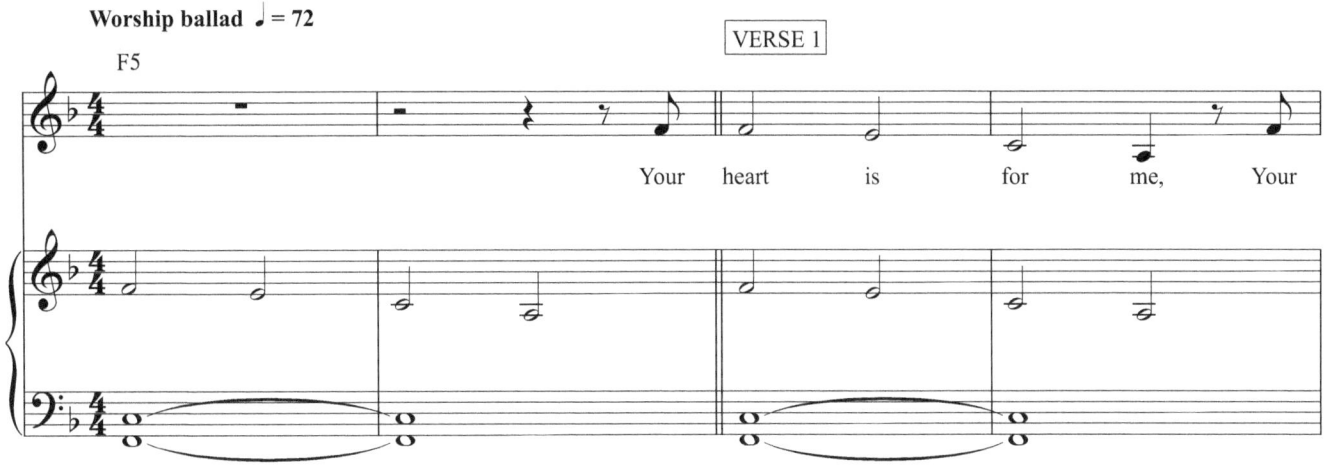

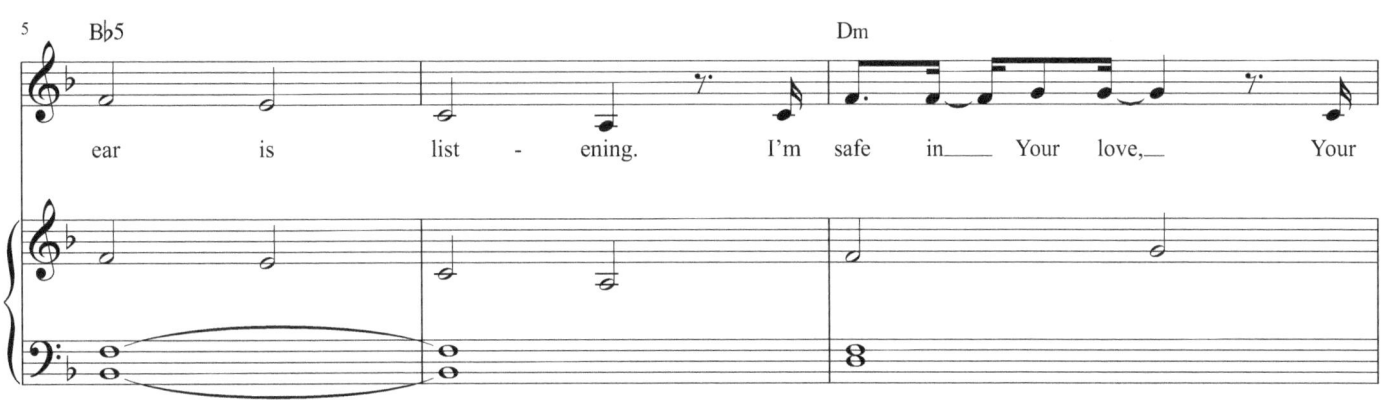

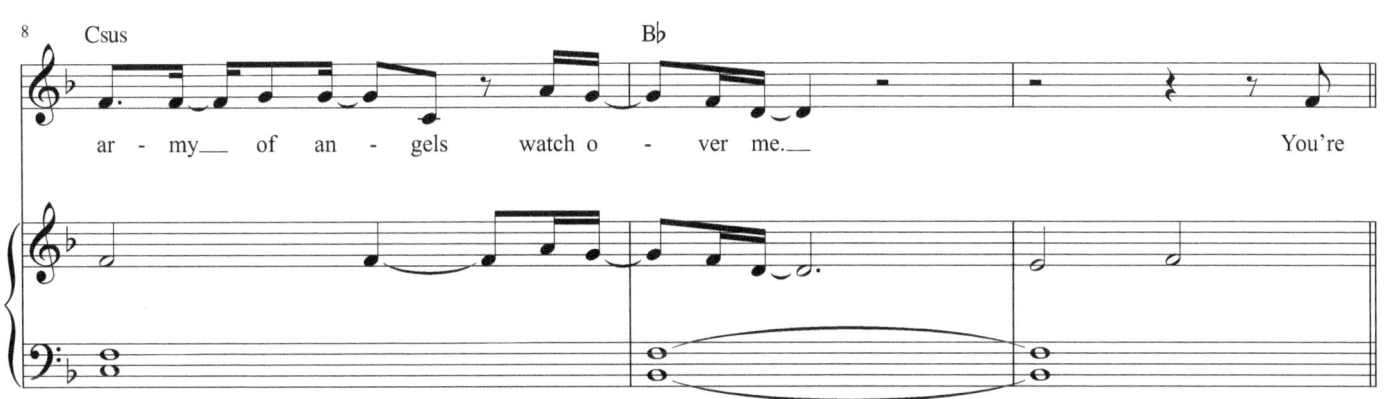

© 2021 Hillsong Music Publishing Australia & Bethel Music Publishing (ASCAP). CCLI: 7177342
All rights reserved. International copyright secured. Used by permission.
Tel: +61 2 8853 5284 Email: publishing@hillsong.com

2.
TAG
43 Dm7 C B♭ F/A
al - ways will be. You are faith - ful and You
45 Dm7 C
al - ways will be. I have nev - er walked a - lone,
CHORUS
47 F Dm7 C
I've nev - er been a - ban - doned. You are my in -
49 B♭sus2 F/A Dm7 C
he - ri - tance, You are my strength and shield. And I have con -
51 F Dm7 C
- fi - dence You go be - fore me. You're my de -
53 B♭sus2 F/A Dm7 C
liv - er - er, I know I nev - er walk a - lone.
CHORUS
55 F Dm7 C
I've nev - er been a - ban - doned. You are my in -
57 B♭sus2 F/A Dm7 C
he - ri - tance, You are my strength and shield. And I have con -

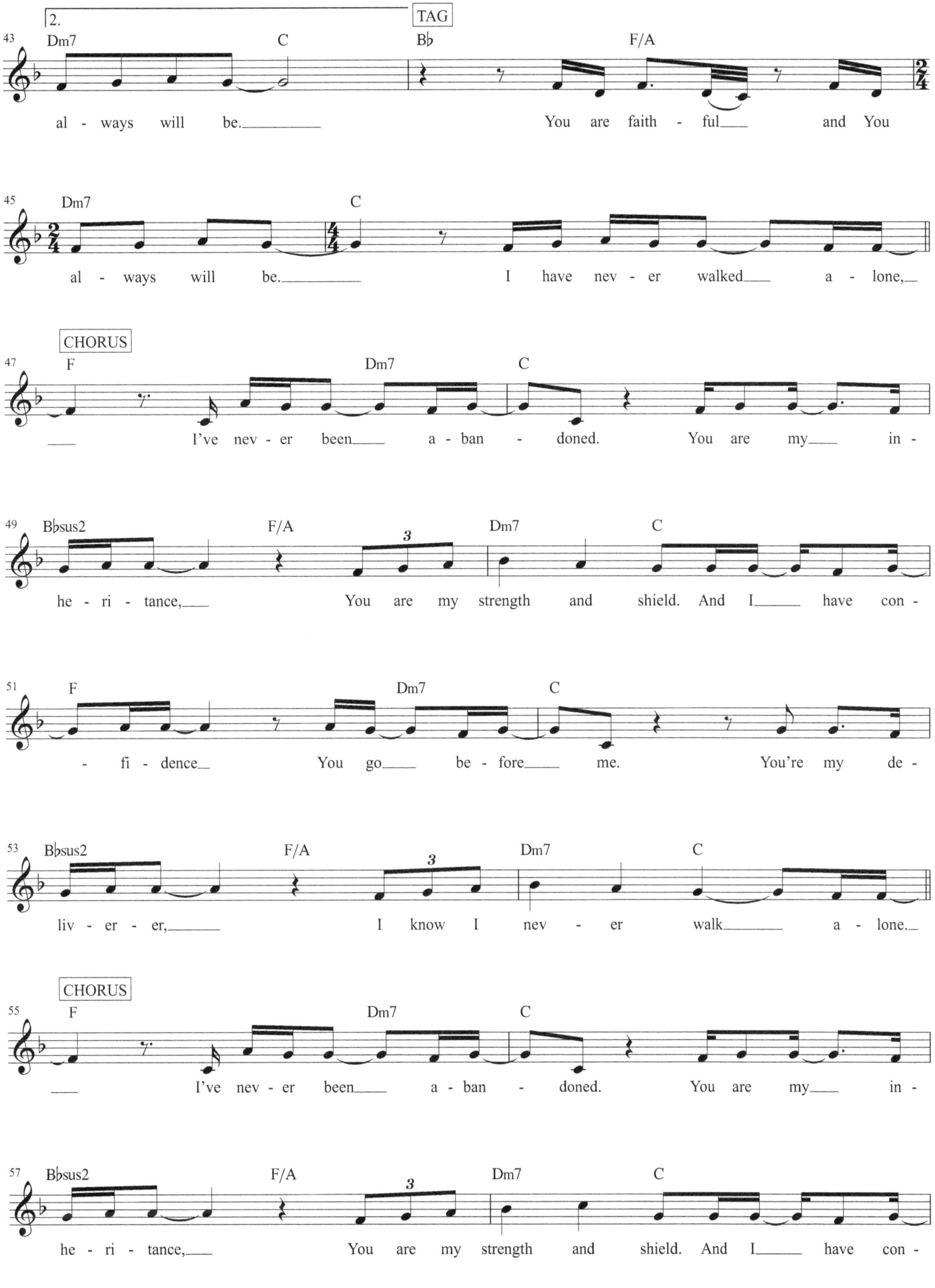

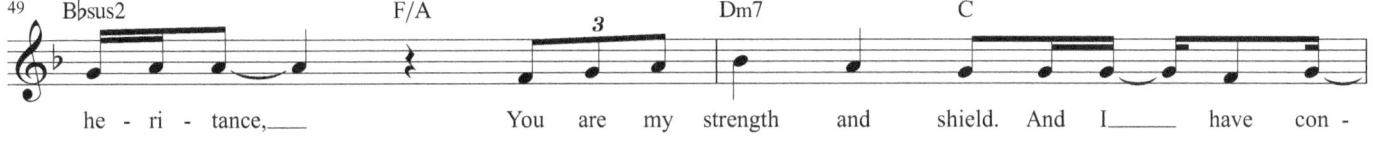

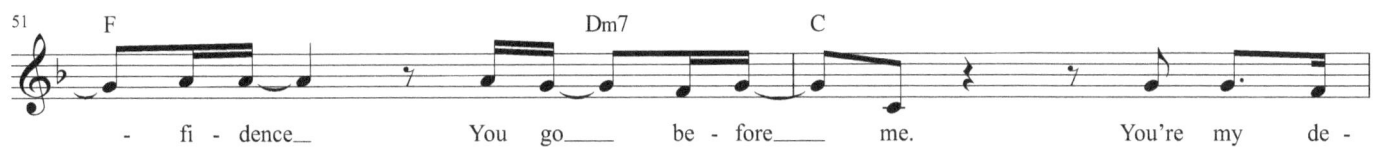

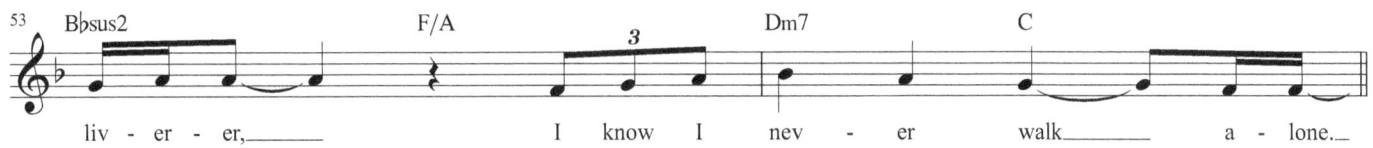

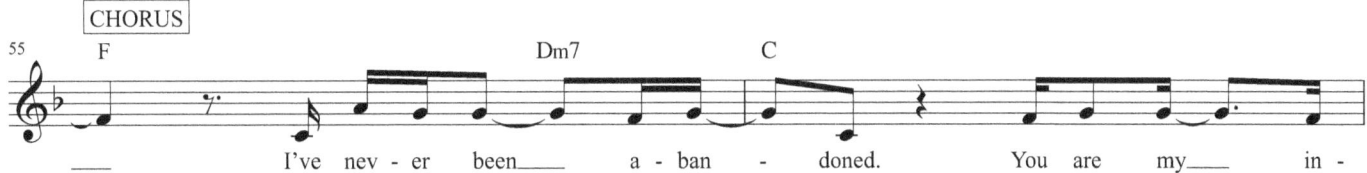

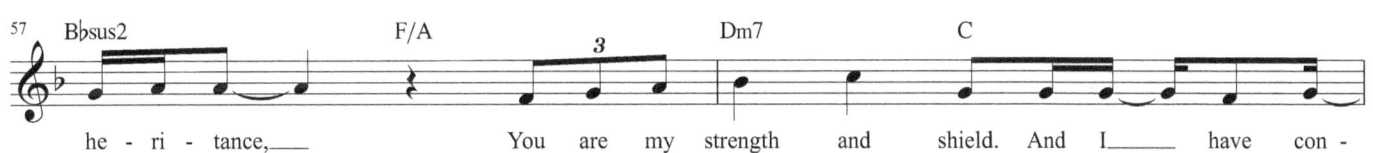

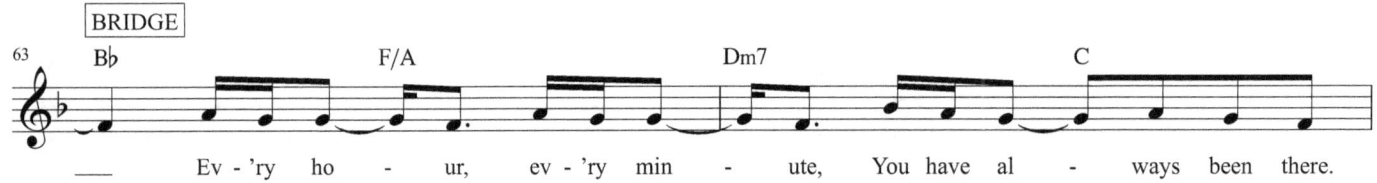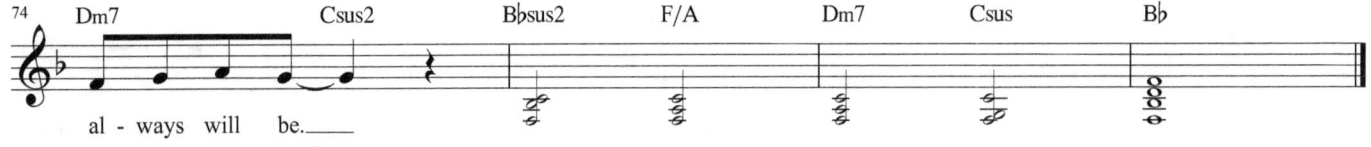

NEVER WALK ALONE

**Words and Music by
Ben Fielding, Hannah Hobbs & Jenn Johnson**

VERSE 1:
Your heart is for me
Your ear is listening
I'm safe in Your love
Your army of angels
Watch over me

VERSE 2:
You're always present
You're always with me
For all of my life
Your favour has followed
You're my covering

CHORUS:
I have never walked alone
I've never been abandoned
You are my inheritance
You are my strength and shield
And I have confidence

© 2021 Hillsong Music Publishing Australia & Bethel Music Publishing (ASCAP)
CCLI: 7177342

PO Box 1195 Castle Hill NSW 1765
Ph: +61 2 8853 5284 Fx: +61 2 8846 4625
E-mail: publishing@hillsong.com

You go before me
You're my deliverer
I know I never walk alone

VERSE 3:
You're always faithful
You're strong and able
I'm lifting my head
In You I find help
You're my providence

BRIDGE:
Every hour
Every minute
You have always been there
You are faithful
And You always will be

In every triumph
Every failure
You are loyal to me
You are faithful
And You always will be

© 2021 Hillsong Music Publishing Australia & Bethel Music Publishing (ASCAP)
CCLI: 7177342

PO Box 1195 Castle Hill NSW 1765
Ph: +61 2 8853 5284 Fx: +61 2 8846 4625
E-mail: publishing@hillsong.com

RESURRENDER

Words and Music by
CHRIS DAVENPORT &
BROOKE LIGERTWOOD

© 2021 Hillsong MP Songs & Hillsong Music Publishing Australia. CCLI: 7184447
All rights reserved. International copyright secured. Used by permission.
Tel: +61 2 8853 5284 Email: publishing@hillsong.com

RESURRENDER

**Words and Music by
CHRIS DAVENPORT &
BROOKE LIGERTWOOD**

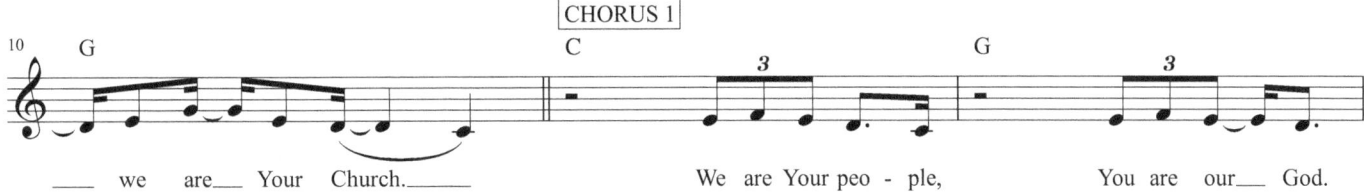

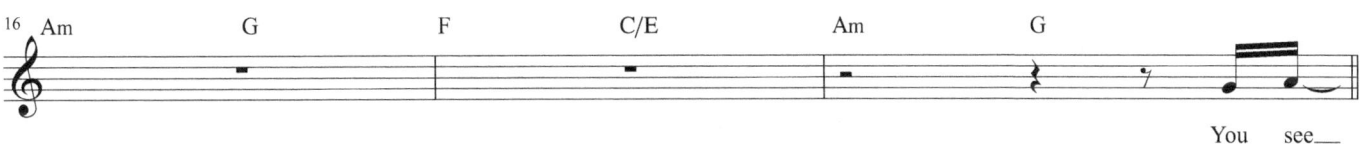

© 2021 Hillsong MP Songs & Hillsong Music Publishing Australia. CCLI: 7184447
All rights reserved. International copyright secured. Used by permission.
Tel: +61 2 8853 5284 Email: publishing@hillsong.com

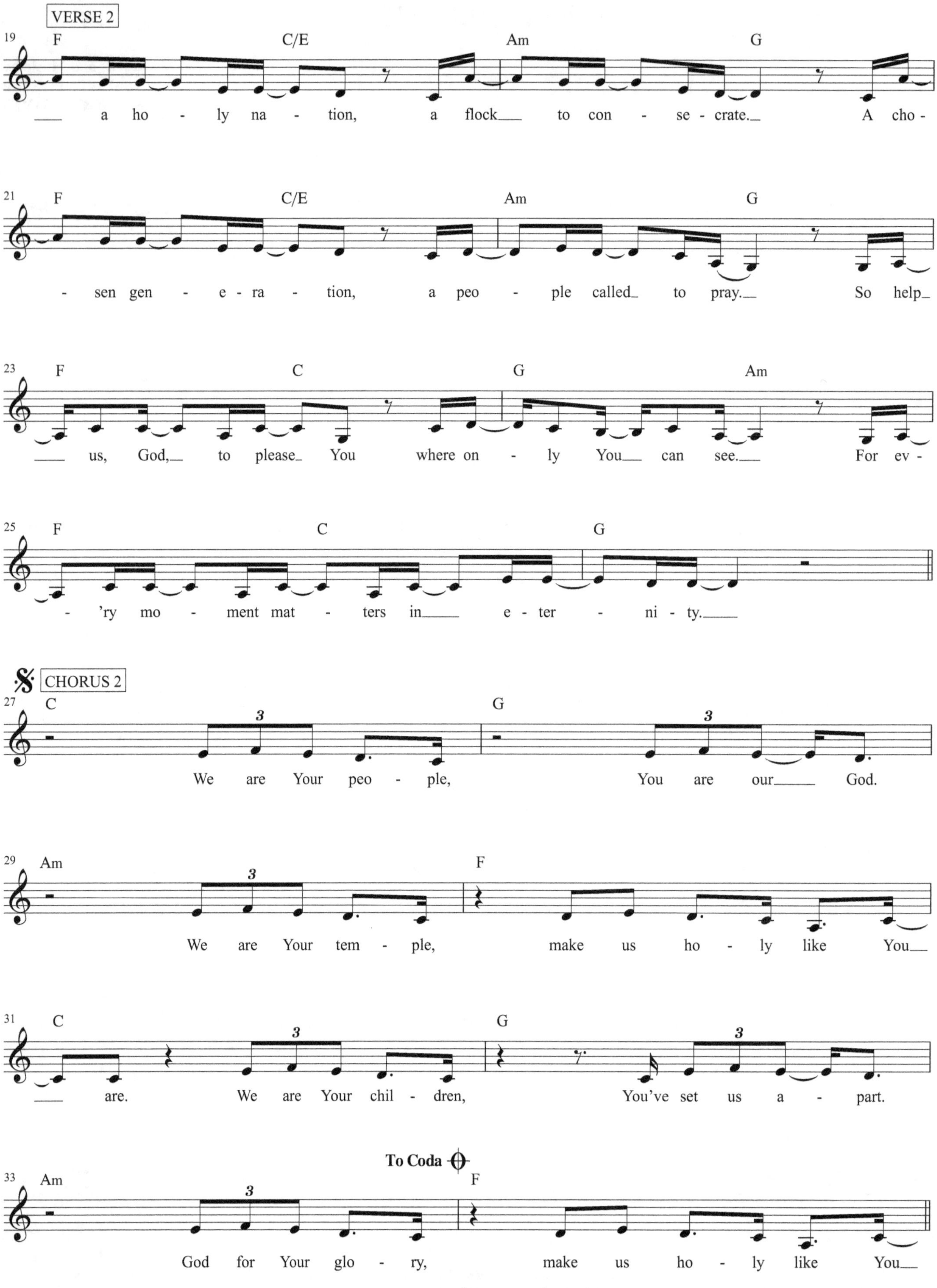
VERSE 2
F C/E Am G
a ho - ly na - tion, a flock to con - se - crate. A cho -
F C/E Am G
- sen gen - e - ra - tion, a peo - ple called to pray. So help
F C G Am
us, God, to please You where on - ly You can see. For ev -
F C G
- 'ry mo - ment mat - ters in e - ter - ni - ty.
CHORUS 2
C G
We are Your peo - ple, You are our God.
Am F
We are Your tem - ple, make us ho - ly like You
C G
are. We are Your chil - dren, You've set us a - part.
To Coda
Am F
God for Your glo - ry, make us ho - ly like You

RESURRENDER

**Words and Music by
Chris Davenport & Brooke Ligertwood**

VERSE 1:
You're turning over tables
And calling for return
To our lives upon the altar
The things we did at first
You're clearing out the temple
You're cleaning out the dirt
For we are Your territory
Lord we are Your Church

CHORUS:
We are Your people
You are our God
We are Your temple
Make us holy like You are

© 2021 Hillsong MP Songs & Hillsong Music Publishing
Australia
CCLI: 7184447

PO Box 1195 Castle Hill NSW 1765
Ph: +61 2 8853 5284 Fx: +61 2 8846 4625
E-mail: publishing@hillsong.com

Resurrender – Page 2

VERSE 2:
You see a holy nation
A flock to consecrate
A chosen generation
A people called to pray
So help us God to please You
Where only You can see
For every moment matters in eternity

CHORUS 2:
We are Your people
You are our God
We are Your temple
Make us holy like You are

We are Your children
You've set us apart
God for Your glory
Make us holy like You are

BRIDGE 1:
Mark Your people with Your presence
Make us a place where You delight to dwell
May we heed Your hand's correction
Oh Lord our Shepherd
You do all things well

© 2021 Hillsong MP Songs & Hillsong Music Publishing Australia
CCLI: 7184447

PO Box 1195 Castle Hill NSW 1765
Ph: +61 2 8853 5284 Fx: +61 2 8846 4625
E-mail: publishing@hillsong.com

Your love as firm as it is tender
Your law is perfect
And Your judgments true
As we run to resurrender
You will restore what we return to You
You are restoring as we yield anew

BRIDGE 2:
If You're calling
We're coming
We're not walking
We're running
God we need resurrender
We resurrender

© 2021 Hillsong MP Songs & Hillsong Music Publishing
Australia
CCLI: 7184447

PO Box 1195 Castle Hill NSW 1765
Ph: +61 2 8853 5284 Fx: +61 2 8846 4625
E-mail: publishing@hillsong.com

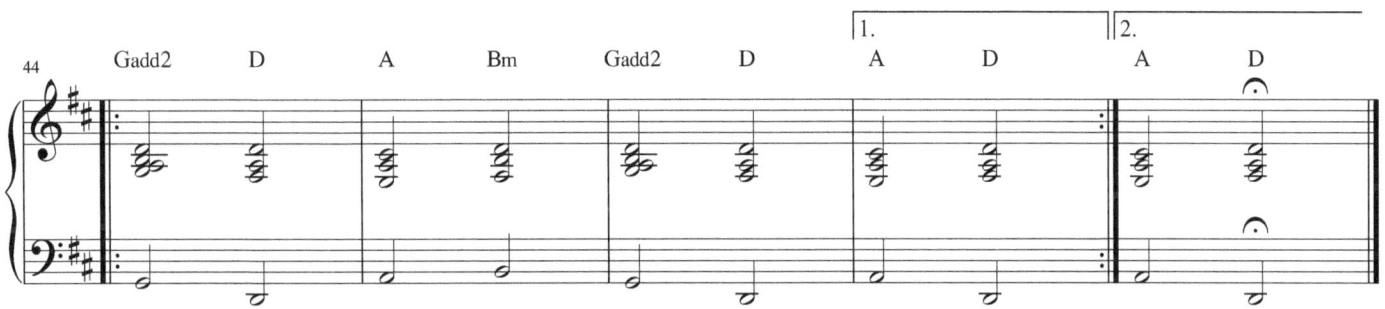

SECRET PLACE

Words and Music by
CHRIS DAVENPORT

© 2021 Hillsong MP Songs. CCLI: 7184446
All rights reserved. International copyright secured. Used by permission.
Tel: +61 2 8853 5284 Email: publishing@hillsong.com

SECRET PLACE

Words and Music by Chris Davenport

VERSE 1:
I remember the beginning
When I found the secret place
Don't know why it felt familiar
But I knew it right away
There were times it seemed so simple
And sometimes so unsure
But not a moment was ever wasted
Knelt behind those closed doors

VERSE 2:
'Cause the secret place is secret
That's where it gets its name
It's not hiding but it's hidden
Far from all religious games
No it won't bring recognition
Or get called up on a stage
'Cause the melody is sacred
You sing in the secret place

© 2021 Hillsong MP Songs
CCLI: 7184446

PO Box 1195 Castle Hill NSW 1765
Ph: +61 2 8853 5284 Fx: +61 2 8846 4625
E-mail: publishing@hillsong.com

VERSE 3:
It's an open invitation
No words you have to say
If you want it you can get there
There's a thousand different ways
There's no glory in the method
None are right and none are wrong
You just put your trust in Jesus
And then start to sing along

VERSE 4:
'Cause just as you are you're welcome
There's no part you have to play
Doesn't need to be impressive
Couldn't do that anyway
'Cause when it gets too complicated
That melody will fade
But if you take the time to listen
You can hear heaven's refrain

© 2021 Hillsong MP Songs
CCLI: 7184446

PO Box 1195 Castle Hill NSW 1765
Ph: +61 2 8853 5284 Fx: +61 2 8846 4625
E-mail: publishing@hillsong.com

VERSE 5:
There'll be days that it feels distant
So far beyond my reach
Like my failures locked the entrance
And my spirit lost the keys
But the beauty of the secret
That I'm so grateful for
Is that Your presence doesn't need me
To kick down an open door

VERSE 6:
So I'm running to the secret
I'm going there today
Got no reason not to worship
And get undignified again
There's no time for inhibitions
Or to care what people say
I won't waste another minute
Take me to the secret place

© 2021 Hillsong MP Songs
CCLI: 7184446

PO Box 1195 Castle Hill NSW 1765
Ph: +61 2 8853 5284 Fx: +61 2 8846 4625
E-mail: publishing@hillsong.com

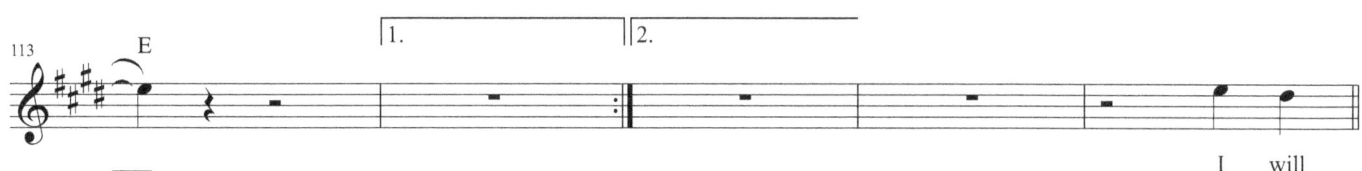

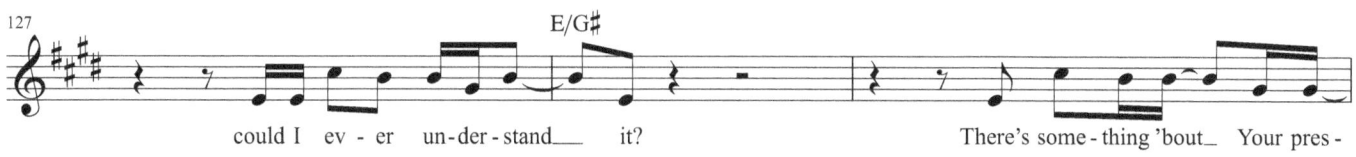

SONG FOR HIS PRESENCE

**Words and Music by
Aodhan King, Ben Tan, Melodie Wagner & Karina Savage**

VERSE 1:
I've heard of wonders
Ancient mysteries
The things of heaven
My eyes have never seen
I wanna know it
Would You make it real for me

VERSE 2:
I've read the stories
With faith and I believe
You're still restoring
Redeeming everything
Here in this moment
May Your will be done in me

PRE-CHORUS:
I will run
Like a child to their mother
To the safety of the Father
To the place where I belong

© 2021 Hillsong Music Publishing Australia
CCLI: 7179142

PO Box 1195 Castle Hill NSW 1765
Ph: +61 2 8853 5284 Fx: +61 2 8846 4625
E-mail: publishing@hillsong.com

Lord Your love
Could I ever understand it
There's something about Your presence
That leaves me wanting more

VERSE 3:
So I'll bring my burdens and insecurities
Run to the throne room and fall down at Your feet
I won't waste a moment
For You have come to set me free

CHORUS:
Let the rain fall down from heaven
Let it wash away the pain
As we worship and surrender
In the triumph of His Name
Feel the weight fall off our shoulders
As our hearts respond in praise
To the God who reigns forever
And ever amen

BRIDGE:
Holy holy holy holy
Is the Lord our God Almighty
One who was and is and is to come

© 2021 Hillsong Music Publishing Australia
CCLI: 7179142

PO Box 1195 Castle Hill NSW 1765
Ph: +61 2 8853 5284 Fx: +61 2 8846 4625
E-mail: publishing@hillsong.com

ALL TO HIM

**Words and Music by
JOEL HOUSTON**

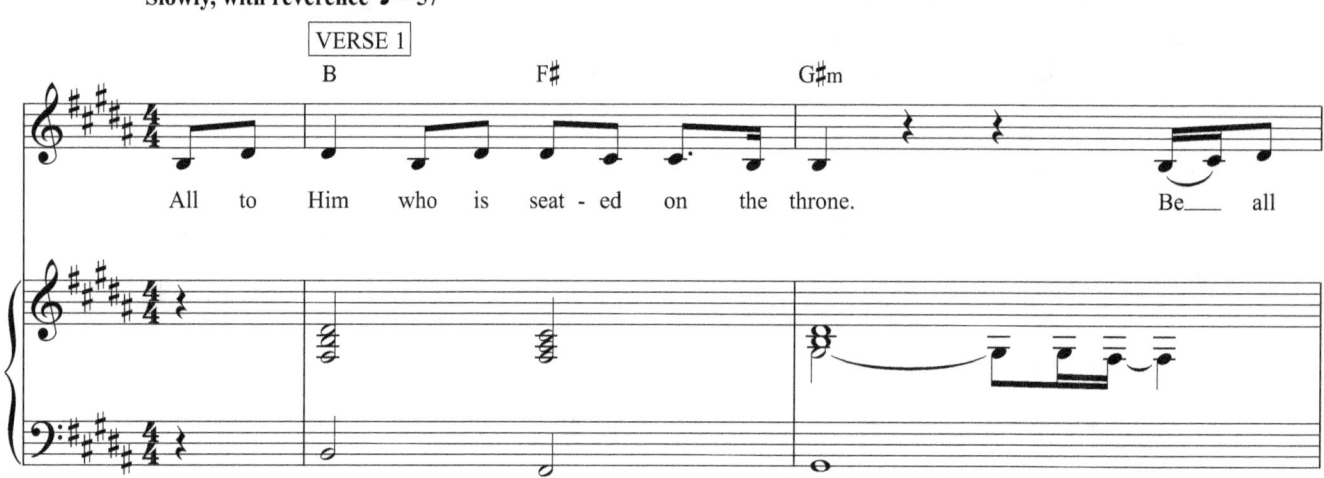

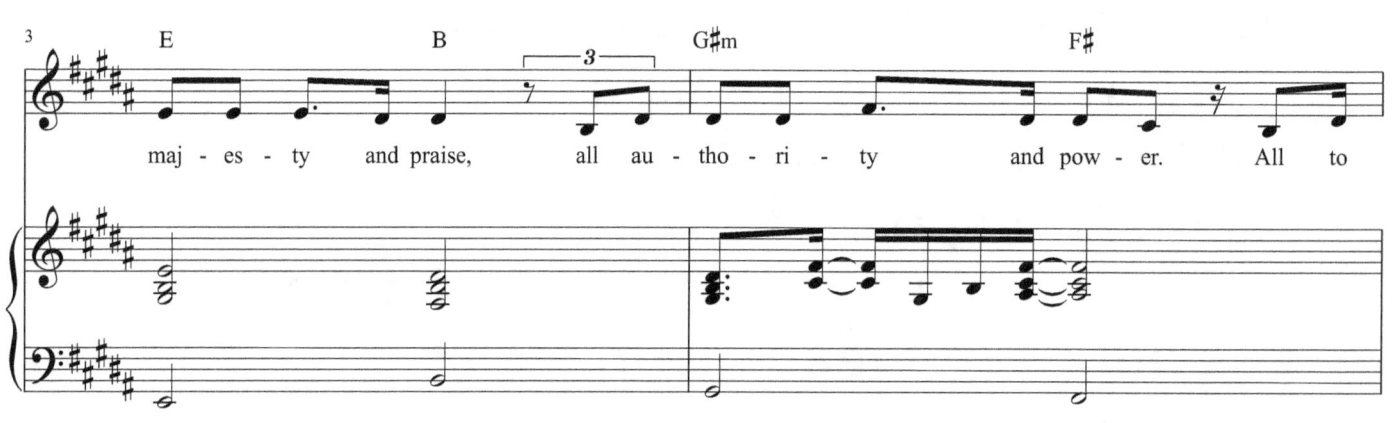

© 2021 Hillsong Music Publishing Australia. CCLI: 7184449
All rights reserved. International copyright secured. Used by permission.
Tel: +61 2 8853 5284 Email: publishing@hillsong.com

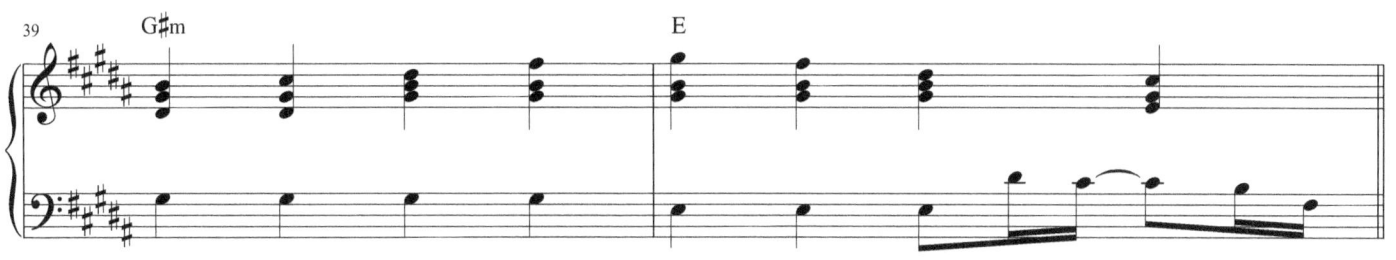

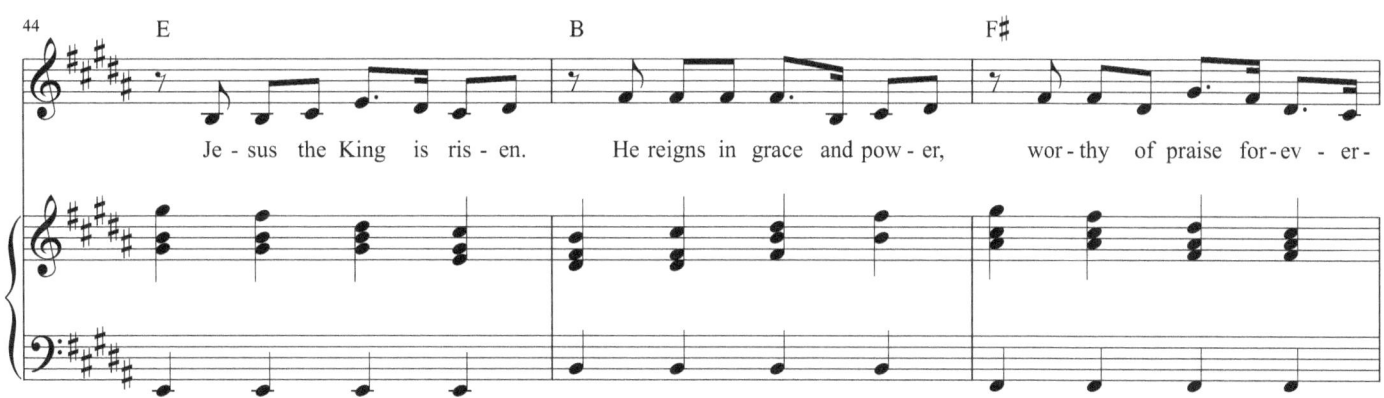
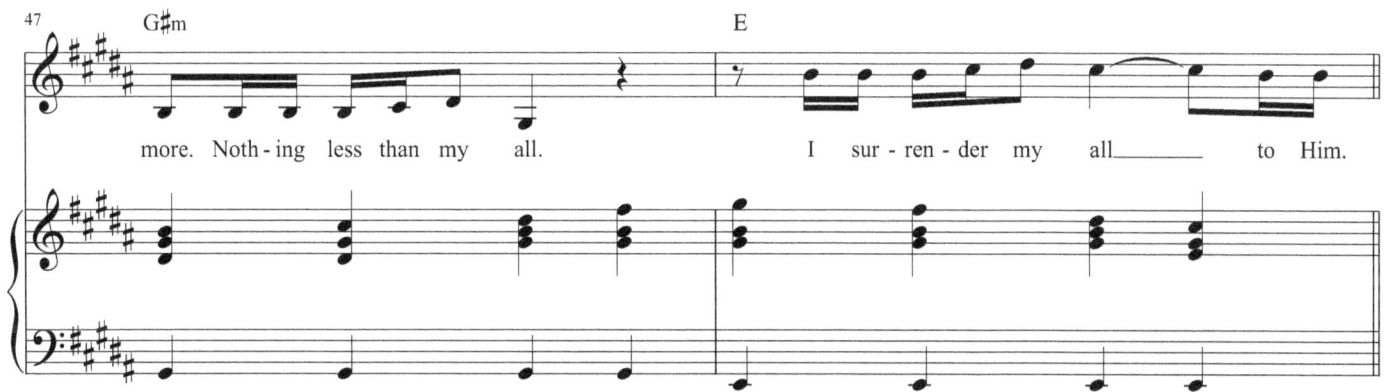

ALL TO HIM

**Words and Music by
JOEL HOUSTON**

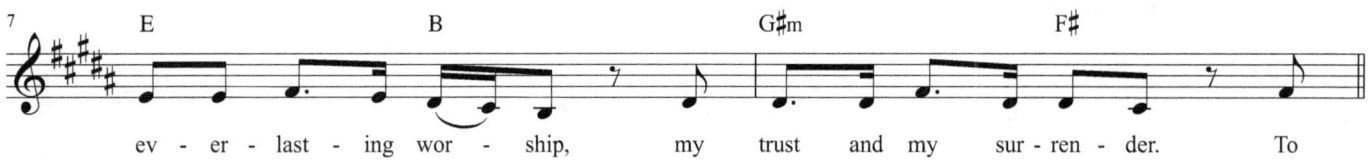
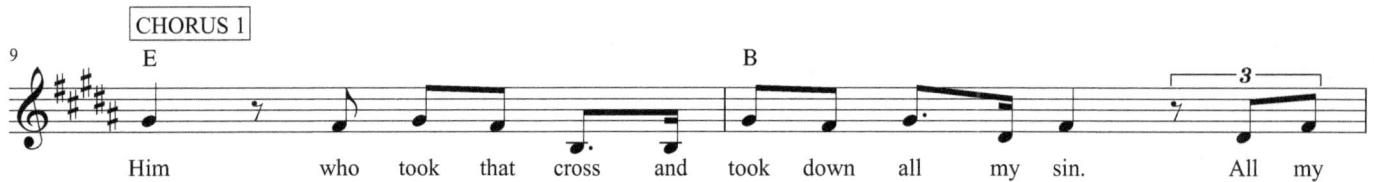

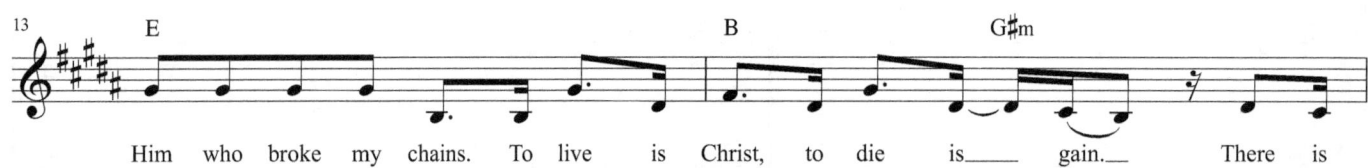

© 2021 Hillsong Music Publishing Australia. CCLI: 7184449
All rights reserved. International copyright secured. Used by permission.
Tel: +61 2 8853 5284 Email: publishing@hillsong.com

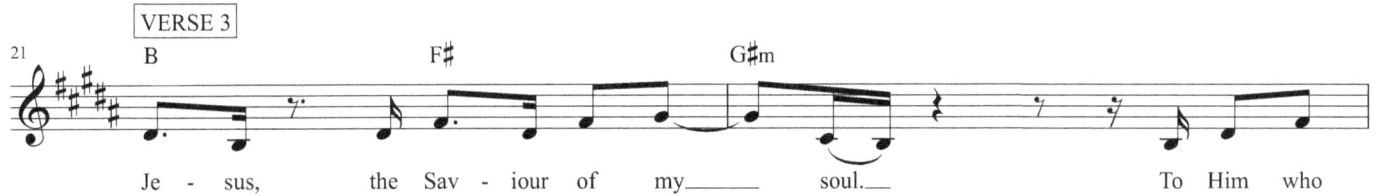
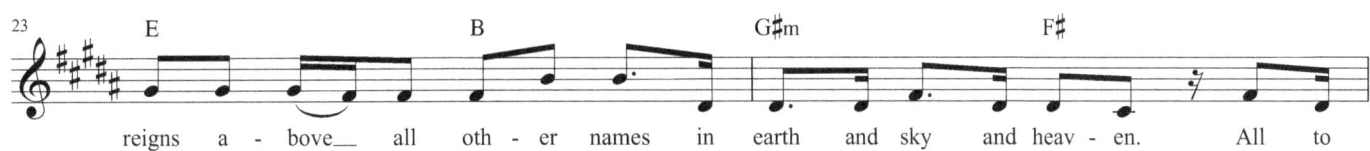

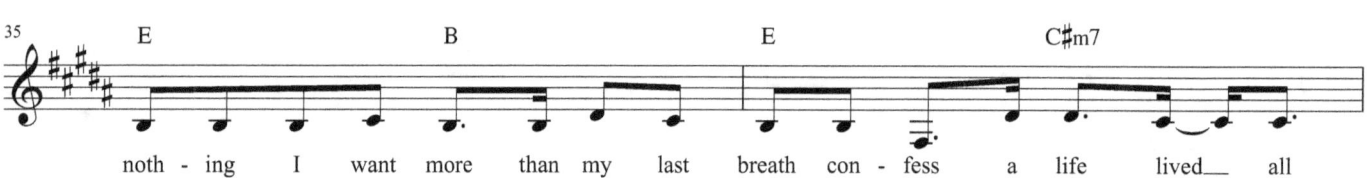

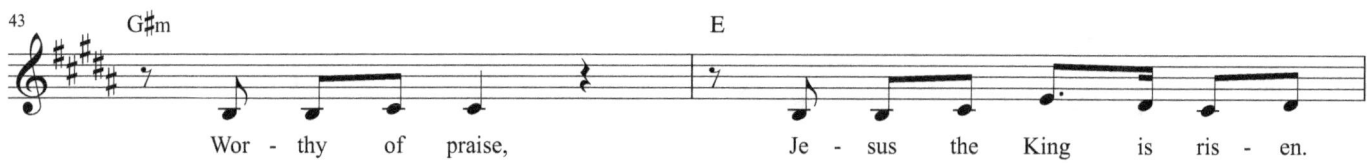
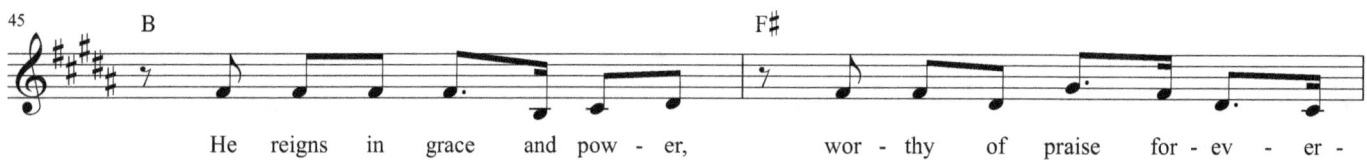
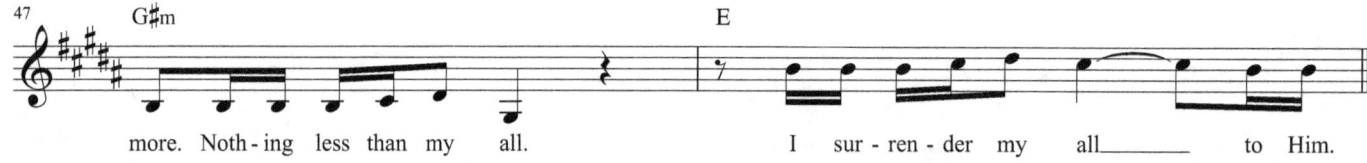

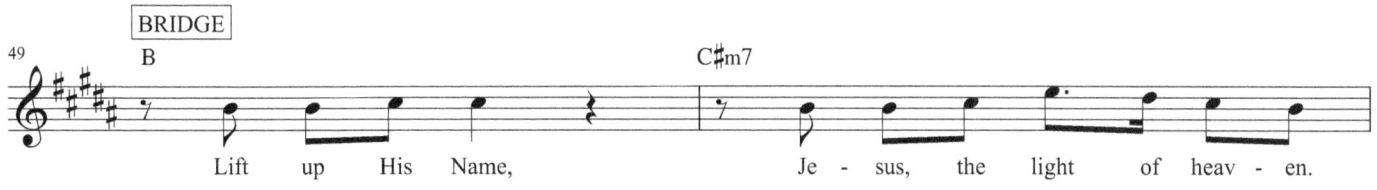
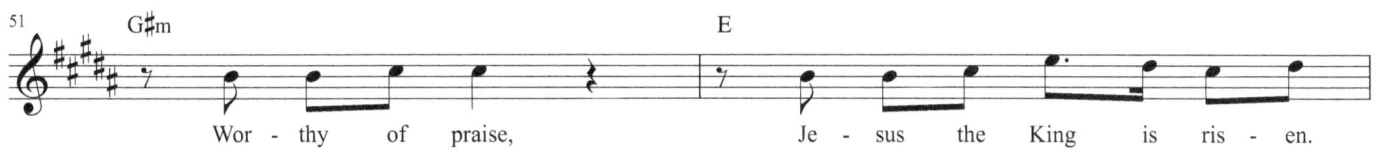
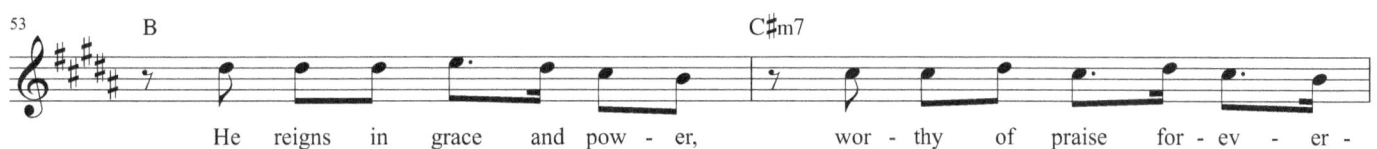
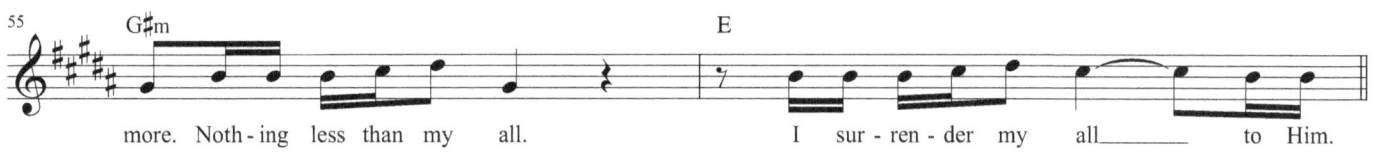
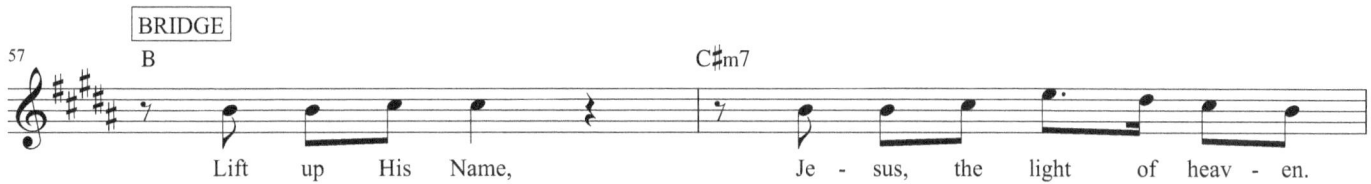
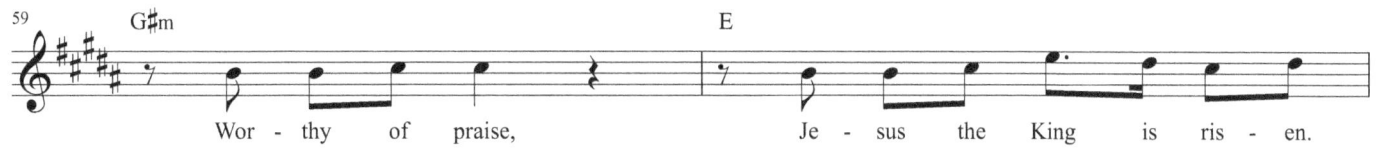

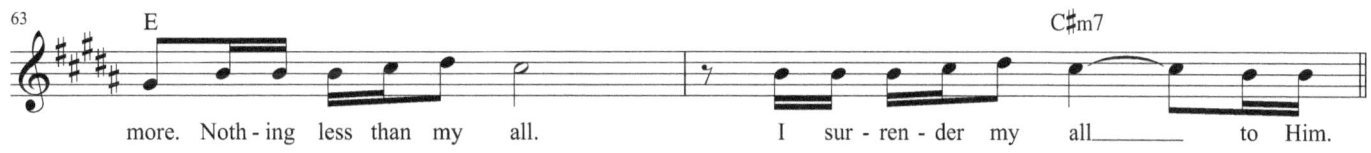

ALL TO HIM

Words and Music by Joel Houston

VERSE 1:
All to Him
Who is seated on the throne
Be all majesty and praise
All authority and power

VERSE 2:
All to Him
Who calls my heart His home
Be my everlasting worship
My trust and my surrender

CHORUS:
To Him
Who took that cross
And took down all my sin
All my shame I bring
All my soul will sing

To Him
Who broke my chains
To live is Christ

© 2021 Hillsong Music Publishing Australia
CCLI: 7184449

PO Box 1195 Castle Hill NSW 1765
Ph: +61 2 8853 5284 Fx: +61 2 8846 4625
E-mail: publishing@hillsong.com

To die is gain
There is nothing I want more
Than my last breath confess
A life lived all to Him

VERSE 3:
All to Jesus
The Saviour of my soul
To Him who reigns above all other names
In earth and sky and heaven

VERSE 4:
All to Jesus
And His praise forevermore
For He kept His word
And He shall return
To sweep up His bride in glory

CHORUS 2:
Now to Him
Because He lives
Because He set me free
I will rest my fears
Where I trust my future

To Him
Who reigns beyond that grave

© 2021 Hillsong Music Publishing Australia
CCLI: 7184449

PO Box 1195 Castle Hill NSW 1765
Ph: +61 2 8853 5284 Fx: +61 2 8846 4625
E-mail: publishing@hillsong.com

With grace to carry me home
There is nothing I want more
Than my last breath confess
A life lived all to Jesus

BRIDGE:
Lift up His Name
Jesus the light of heaven
Worthy of praise
Jesus the King is risen
He reigns in grace and power
Worthy of praise forevermore
Nothing less than my all
I surrender my all to Him

ALT-BRIDGE/TAG:
All to Him our God
Who reigns forevermore
Be all the praise
And all the glory
All to Him whose Name
Is worthy of it all
My life to Jesus
I surrender all

© 2021 Hillsong Music Publishing Australia
CCLI: 7184449

PO Box 1195 Castle Hill NSW 1765
Ph: +61 2 8853 5284 Fx: +61 2 8846 4625
E-mail: publishing@hillsong.com

Resources

FOR MORE GREAT RESOURCES,
SCAN THIS QR CODE

OR PLEASE VISIT
hillsongstore.com/thesesameskies

www.ingramcontent.com/pod-product-compliance
Lightning Source LLC
Chambersburg PA
CBHW082101230426
43670CB00017B/2922